all new Cookie Dough Fun

D1304664

Publications International, Ltd.

Favorite Brand Name Recipes at www.fbnr.com

Copyright © 2008 Publications International, Ltd.
All rights reserved. This publication may not be reproduced or quoted in whole or in part by any means whatsoever without written permission from:

Louis Weber, CEO
Publications International, Ltd.
7373 North Cicero Avenue
Lincolnwood, IL 60712

Permission is never granted for commercial purposes.

Some of the products listed in this publication may be in limited distribution.

Recipe development on pages 10, 16 left, 22, 23 left, 24, 26 left, 36, 40, 46, 48, 52, 60, 66 and 76 by Kathy Joy.
Recipe development on pages 12, 15 right, 16 right, 18 left, 30, 32, 34, 38, 54, 56 right, 78, 80, 84, 88 and 90 by Alison Reich.
Recipe development on pages 8, 14, 15 left, 20, 28 left, 42, 44, 50, 56 left, 58, 62, 64, 68 and 70 by Susie Skoog.

All photographs *except* those on pages 73 and 75 by Proffitt Photography, Chicago.
Photographer: Laurie Proffitt
Photographer's Assistant: Chad Evans
Prop Stylist: Karen Johnson
Assistant Prop Stylist: Sara H. Yunker
Food Stylist: Kathy Aragaki
Assistant Food Stylist: Lisa Knych

Pictured on the front cover *(clockwise from top left):* Zebra *(page 80),* Banana Split Ice Cream Sandwich *(page 34),* S'More Cup *(page 60)* and Birthday Cake Cookie *(page 78).*

Pictured on the back cover *(top to bottom):* Nothin' But Net *(page 83)* and Snickerpoodles *(page 86).*

ISBN-13: 978-1-4127-2904-8
ISBN-10: 1-4127-2904-1

Manufactured in China.

8 7 6 5 4 3 2 1

Microwave Cooking: Microwave ovens vary in wattage. Use the cooking times as guidelines and check for doneness before adding more time.

all new Cookie Dough Fun

Basic Cookie Tips

• Read the entire recipe before beginning to make sure you have all the necessary baking utensils and ingredients.

• Unless otherwise directed in the recipe, all purchased cookie dough should be well chilled before using. Work with the recommended portion of dough called for and refrigerate the remaining dough until needed.

• Most purchased cookie dough expands considerably when baked. Always leave 2 inches between unbaked cookies when placing them on the cookie sheet, unless the recipe directs otherwise.

• Follow the recipe directions and baking times exactly. Check for doneness using the test given in the recipe. Most cookies bake quickly, so check them at the minimum baking time, then watch carefully to make sure they don't burn.

Making Patterns for Cutouts

When a pattern for a cutout cookie is to be used only once, make the pattern out of waxed paper. Using the diagram or photo as a guide, draw the pattern pieces on waxed paper; cut out and place on the rolled-out dough. Cut around the pattern pieces with a sharp knife. Remove the pattern pieces and discard. Continue as directed in the recipe. For patterns that are to be used more than once, use clean, lightweight cardboard or poster board. Using the diagram or photo as a guide, draw the pattern pieces on the cardboard; cut out and lightly spray one side with nonstick cooking spray. Place the pattern pieces, sprayed side down, on the rolled-out dough; cut around them with a sharp knife. Reuse the pattern pieces to make as many cutouts as needed.

Decorating Ideas

Chocolate Drizzle
Drizzle melted semisweet, milk or white chocolate over baked goods.

Powdered Sugar Glaze
Mix 1 cup sifted powdered sugar and 5 teaspoons milk in a small bowl. Add $1/2$ teaspoon vanilla extract or other flavoring, if desired. Stir until smooth; tint with food coloring, if desired. If the glaze is too thin, add additional

sifted powdered sugar; if it is too thick, add additional milk, 1/2 teaspoon at a time.

Toasted Nuts or Coconut

To toast, spread nuts or flaked coconut in a thin layer on an ungreased cookie sheet. Bake in a preheated 325°F oven 7 to 10 minutes or until golden, stirring occasionally. Toasted nuts will become darker and crisper as they cool. Always allow nuts to cool before using.

Tinted Coconut

To tint coconut, dilute a few drops of liquid food coloring with 1/2 teaspoon milk or water in a small bowl. Add 1 to 1 1/3 cups flaked coconut; toss with a fork until evenly tinted.

Melting Chocolate

Make sure the utensils you use for melting chocolate are completely dry. Moisture makes chocolate become stiff and grainy. If this happens, add 1/2 teaspoon shortening (not butter) for each ounce of chocolate; stir until smooth. Chocolate scorches easily and cannot be used once scorched. Use one of the following methods for successful melting.

Double Boiler: This is the safest method because it prevents scorching. Place the chocolate in the top of a double boiler or in a bowl over hot, not boiling, water; stir until smooth. (Make sure the water remains just below a simmer and is 1 inch below the top pan.) Be careful that no steam or water gets into the chocolate.

Direct Heat: Place the chocolate in a heavy saucepan and melt it over very low heat, stirring constantly. Remove the chocolate from the heat as soon as it is melted. Chocolate is easily scorched with this method.

Microwave Oven: Place 4 to 6 unwrapped 1-ounce squares of chocolate or 1 cup of chocolate chips in a small microwavable bowl. Microwave on HIGH for 1 to 1 1/2 minutes. Stir after 1 minute and at 30-second intervals after the first minute. Repeat the procedure as necessary to melt the chocolate. Be sure to stir the microwaved chocolate because it can retain its original shape even when melted.

Cookie Dough Delights

Natty Tropical Cookies

1 package (18 ounces) refrigerated chocolate chip and caramel cookie dough
2 cups flaked coconut
1½ cups macadamia nuts, chopped
1 to 1½ tablespoons freshly grated orange peel

1. Preheat oven to 350°F. Lightly grease cookie sheets. Let dough stand at room temperature about 15 minutes.

2. Combine dough, coconut, nuts and orange peel in large bowl; beat until well blended. Shape dough into 1¼-inch balls; place 2 inches apart on prepared cookie sheets.

3. Bake about 15 minutes or until edges are brown and centers are set. Cool 2 minutes on cookie sheets. Remove to wire racks; cool completely.

Makes about 30 cookies

Natty Tropical Cookies

Key Lime Tartlets

1 package (18 ounces) refrigerated sugar cookie dough

½ cup finely chopped pecans

1 can (14 ounces) sweetened condensed milk

¼ cup plus 1 tablespoon bottled key lime juice

1 teaspoon freshly grated lime peel

Aerosol whipped topping, additional freshly grated lime peel and lime wedge candies

1. Preheat oven to 350°F. Lightly grease 18 standard (2½-inch) muffin pan cups or line with paper or foil baking cups. Let cookie dough stand at room temperature about 15 minutes.

2. Combine dough and pecans in large bowl; beat until well blended. Shape dough into 18 balls; press onto bottoms and up sides of prepared muffin cups.

3. Bake 12 to 15 minutes or until set. Remove from oven; gently press down center of each cookie cup with back of teaspoon. Cool in pan for 10 minutes. Remove cups from pans; cool completely on wire rack.

4. Combine sweetened condensed milk, juice and peel in small bowl; stir until well blended. Divide evenly among cooled cookie cups. Garnish with whipped topping, lime peel and lime candies.

Makes 18 tartlets

When grating lime peel, grate only the outer green layer, which is sweet and flavorful. Avoid grating into the white pith, as it has a bitter taste.

Key Lime Tartlets

Sweet Jam Swirls

1 package (18 ounces) refrigerated sugar cookie dough

1 package (8 ounces) cream cheese, softened

¾ cup all-purpose flour

¼ cup jam (any flavor)

¼ cup granulated sugar or coarse decorating sugar

1. Let dough stand at room temperature about 15 minutes.

2. Combine sugar cookie dough, cream cheese and flour in large bowl; beat until well blended. Divide dough into 4 equal pieces; wrap each piece tightly in plastic wrap. Freeze 1 hour.

3. Working with one dough piece, roll into 5×5-inch square on floured waxed paper. Spread 1 tablespoon jam evenly over dough square. Roll up into log; wrap tightly in plastic wrap. Repeat with remaining dough pieces and jam. Freeze logs about 3 hours or until firm.

4. Preheat oven to 350°F. Lightly grease cookie sheets. Cut dough logs into ¼-inch slices; place 2 inches apart on prepared cookie sheets. Sprinkle evenly with sugar.

5. Bake 9 to 11 minutes or until edges are lightly browned. Cool on cookie sheets 1 minute. Remove to wire racks; cool completely.

Makes about 60 cookies

Sweet Jam Swirls

Double Cherry Crumbles

½ **(18-ounce) package refrigerated oatmeal raisin cookie dough***

½ **cup uncooked old-fashioned oats**

¾ **teaspoon ground cinnamon**

½ **teaspoon ground ginger**

2 **tablespoons cold butter, cut into small pieces**

1 **cup chopped pecans, toasted****

1 **bag (16 ounces) frozen pitted unsweetened dark sweet cherries, thawed**

2 **cans (21 ounces each) cherry pie filling**

*Save remaining ½ package of dough for another use.

**To toast pecans, spread in single layer on baking sheet. Bake in preheated 350°F oven 7 to 10 minutes or until golden brown, stirring frequently.

1. Preheat oven to 350°F. Lightly grease 8 (½-cup) ramekins; place on cookie sheet. Let half package of dough stand at room temperature about 15 minutes.

2. For topping, combine dough, uncooked oats, cinnamon and ginger in large bowl. Beat until well blended. Cut in butter with pastry blender or 2 knives. Stir in pecans; set aside.

3. Combine thawed cherries and pie filling in large bowl; stir until well blended. Divide cherry mixture evenly among prepared ramekins; sprinkle evenly with topping.

4. Bake about 25 minutes or until topping is browned. Cool slightly in ramekins on wire rack. Serve warm or at room temperature.

Makes 8 servings

Peanut Butter Pixies

1 package (18 ounces) refrigerated peanut butter cookie dough
¼ cup all-purpose flour
1½ teaspoons ground cinnamon
¾ teaspoon ground ginger
½ teaspoon ground nutmeg
Granulated sugar

1. Preheat oven to 350°F. Lightly grease cookie sheets. Let dough stand at room temperature about 15 minutes.

2. Combine dough, flour, cinnamon, ginger and nutmeg in large bowl; beat until well blended. Shape dough into ¾-inch balls; roll in sugar. Place balls 1 inch apart on prepared cookie sheets.

3. Bake 7 to 9 minutes or until edges are browned. Cool 2 minutes on cookie sheets. Remove to wire racks; cool completely.

Makes 60 cookies

Apple Cinnamon Chunkies

1 package (18 ounces) refrigerated oatmeal raisin cookie dough
1 cup chopped dried apples
½ cup cinnamon baking chips
½ teaspoon apple pie spice*

*Substitute ¼ teaspoon ground cinnamon, ⅛ teaspoon ground nutmeg and pinch of ground allspice or ground cloves for ½ teaspoon apple pie spice.

1. Preheat oven to 350°F. Lightly grease cookie sheets. Let dough stand at room temperature about 15 minutes.

2. Combine dough, apples, cinnamon chips and spice in large bowl; beat until blended. Drop dough by rounded tablespoonfuls 2 inches apart onto prepared cookie sheets.

3. Bake 10 to 12 minutes or until golden. Cool on cookie sheets 2 to 3 minutes. Remove to wire racks; cool completely.

Makes 24 cookies

Candy Cups

1 package (18 ounces)
  refrigerated sugar
  cookie dough
$\frac{1}{3}$ cup all-purpose flour
1 package (12 ounces)
  bite-sized chocolate-
  covered peanut,
  caramel and nougat
  candy
$\frac{1}{4}$ cup cocktail peanuts,
  chopped

1. Preheat oven to 350°F. Grease 36 mini (1$\frac{3}{4}$-inch) muffin pan cups. Let cookie dough stand at room temperature about 15 minutes.

2. Combine dough and flour in large bowl; beat until well blended. Shape dough into 36 balls; press onto bottoms and up sides of prepared muffin cups. Place 1 candy into center of each muffin cup.

3. Bake 10 to 11 minutes or until edges are golden brown. Immediately sprinkle with peanuts. Cool 10 minutes in pan on wire racks. Remove to wire racks; cool completely.

Makes 36 cookies

Snowball Bites

1 package (18 ounces)
  refrigerated sugar
  cookie dough
$\frac{3}{4}$ cup all-purpose flour
2 tablespoons honey or
  maple syrup
1 cup chopped walnuts
  Powdered sugar

1. Let cookie dough stand at room temperature about 15 minutes. Combine cookie dough, flour and honey in large bowl; beat until well blended. Stir in walnuts. Shape dough into disk; wrap tightly in plastic wrap. Refrigerate dough at least 2 hours or up to 2 days.

2. Preheat oven to 350°F. Place powdered sugar in small shallow bowl; set aside. Shape dough into $\frac{3}{4}$-inch balls; place 1$\frac{1}{2}$ inches apart on ungreased cookie sheets.

3. Bake 10 to 12 minutes or until bottoms are browned. Roll warm cookies in powdered sugar. Cool completely on wire racks. Just before serving, roll cookies in additional powdered sugar, if desired.

Makes about 30 cookies

Candy Cups

Pecan Sables

1 package (18 ounces)
   refrigerated sugar
   cookie dough
½ cup sugar
¼ teaspoon ground
   cinnamon
2 cups finely chopped
   pecans
1½ cups pecan halves

1. Preheat oven to 350°F. Lightly grease cookie sheets. Let dough stand at room temperature about 15 minutes.

2. Combine sugar and cinnamon in small bowl; set aside. Combine dough and chopped pecans in large bowl; beat until well blended.

3. Shape dough into 1-inch balls; roll in cinnamon-sugar. Place balls 2 inches apart on prepared cookie sheets. Press one pecan half into each dough ball.

4. Bake 8 to 10 minutes or until edges are lightly browned. Cool 2 minutes on cookie sheets. Remove to wire racks; cool completely.

Makes 36 cookies

Maple Oatmeal Raisin Drops

1 package (18 ounces)
   refrigerated sugar
   cookie dough
1 cup uncooked quick oats
1 cup raisins
¼ cup maple syrup
   **Prepared powdered sugar
   glaze (optional)**

1. Preheat oven to 350°F. Grease cookie sheets. Let cookie dough stand at room temperature about 15 minutes.

2. Combine dough, oats, raisins and maple syrup in large bowl; beat until well blended. Drop by rounded teaspoonfuls 2 inches apart onto prepared cookie sheets.

3. Bake 9 to 11 minutes or until edges are lightly browned and centers are set. Cool on cookie sheets 1 minute. Remove to wire racks; cool completely.

4. Drizzle glaze over cooled cookies, if desired. Let stand until set. *Makes 36 cookies*

Pecan Sables

Raspberry Buckle Cupcakes

½ (18-ounce) package refrigerated sugar cookie dough*

½ cup all-purpose flour

¼ cup firmly packed light brown sugar

1 teaspoon vanilla

½ cup slivered almonds

1 package (18¼ ounces) lemon cake mix plus ingredients to prepare mix

1 can (12 ounces) raspberry pie filling

*Save remaining ½ package of dough for another use.

1. Preheat oven to 350°F. Line 24 standard (2½-inch) muffin pan cups with paper or foil baking cups.

2. For topping, combine cookie dough, flour, brown sugar and vanilla in large bowl; beat until well blended. Stir in almonds; set aside.

3. Prepare cake mix as directed on package. Divide batter evenly among prepared muffin pan cups; place 1 tablespoon pie filling on batter in each muffin cup. Bake 10 minutes.

4. Sprinkle topping evenly over partially baked cupcakes. Bake 15 minutes or until topping is browned and cupcakes are set.

Makes 24 cupcakes

To easily fill muffin cups, place the batter in a 4-cup glass measure. Using a plastic spatula to control the flow of the batter, fill each cup three-fourths full.

Raspberry Buckle Cupcakes

Banana Oatmeal Caramel Cookies

1 package (18 ounces) refrigerated turtle cookie dough

2 ripe bananas, mashed

1⅓ cups uncooked old-fashioned oats

⅔ cup all-purpose flour

½ cup semisweet chocolate chips

1. Preheat oven to 350°F. Lightly grease cookie sheets. Let dough stand at room temperature about 15 minutes.

2. Combine dough, bananas, oats and flour in large bowl; beat until well blended. Drop dough by heaping tablespoonfuls 2 inches apart onto prepared cookie sheets; flatten slightly.

3. Bake 16 to 18 minutes or until edges are browned and cookies are set. Cool on cookie sheets 1 minute. Remove to wire racks; cool completely.

4. Place chocolate chips in small resealable food storage bag. Microwave on MEDIUM (50%) 1 minute; knead bag lightly. Microwave and knead at additional 30-second intervals until chocolate is completely melted. Cut off tiny corner of bag. Drizzle melted chocolate over cookies. Let stand until set.

Makes about 24 cookies

Variation: Use triple chocolate cookie dough instead of the turtle dough.

Peanut Butter & Jelly Pockets

1 package (18 ounces) refrigerated peanut butter cookie dough
1 jar (10 ounces) strawberry or raspberry pastry filling
Coarse decorating sugar

1. Freeze dough 1 hour or until completely firm.

2. Preheat oven to 350°F. Lightly grease cookie sheets.

3. Cut dough into ¼-inch slices; place half of dough slices 2 inches apart on prepared cookie sheets. Spoon about 1 teaspoon pastry filling each onto centers of dough slices; top with remaining dough slices. Sprinkle tops with decorating sugar.

4. Bake 12 to 15 minutes or until edges are lightly browned. Cool on cookie sheets 3 minutes. Remove to wire racks; cool completely.

Makes about 18 cookies

Coconut Craters

1 package (18 ounces) refrigerated chocolate chip cookie dough
¼ cup packed brown sugar
2 tablespoons milk
1 tablespoon butter, melted
1 cup flaked coconut
½ cup chocolate-covered toffee baking bits

1. Preheat oven to 350°F. Line 36 mini (1¾-inch) muffin pan cups with paper baking cups.

2. Shape dough into 36 balls; press onto bottoms and up sides of muffin cups. Bake 9 to 11 minutes or until golden.

3. Meanwhile, combine brown sugar, milk and butter in medium bowl. Stir in coconut and toffee bits. Gently press down center of each cookie cup with back of teaspoon. Spoon 1 rounded teaspoon toffee mixture into each cup. Bake 2 to 4 minutes or until golden. Cool in pan 10 minutes. Remove to wire racks; cool completely.

Makes 36 cookies

Spicy Molasses Cookies

1 package (18 ounces) refrigerated oatmeal raisin cookie dough
½ cup all-purpose flour
¼ cup molasses
1 teaspoon ground ginger
1 teaspoon ground cinnamon
¼ teaspoon ground cloves
1 cup powdered sugar
2 tablespoons milk

1. Preheat oven to 350°F. Lightly grease cookie sheets. Let cookie dough stand at room temperature about 15 minutes.

2. Combine cookie dough, flour, molasses, ginger, cinnamon and cloves in large bowl; beat at medium speed of electric mixer until well blended. Drop dough by rounded tablespoonfuls 2 inches apart onto prepared cookie sheets.

3. Bake 10 to 12 minutes or until centers are set. Cool on cookie sheets 1 minute. Remove to wire racks; cool completely.

4. Combine powdered sugar and milk in small bowl; stir until smooth; add additional milk, if necessary, until desired drizzling consistency is reached. Drizzle icing over cooled cookies; let stand until set.

Makes about 24 cookies

Before measuring molasses, lightly coat the measuring cup with nonstick cooking spray so the molasses will slide out easily instead of clinging to the cup.

Spicy Molasses Cookies

Toffee Chipsters

1 package (18 ounces)
   refrigerated sugar
   cookie dough
1 cup white chocolate chips
1 bag (8 ounces) chocolate-
   covered toffee baking
   bits, divided

1. Preheat oven to 350°F. Lightly grease cookie sheets. Let dough stand at room temperature about 15 minutes.

2. Combine dough, white chocolate chips and 1 cup toffee bits in large bowl; beat until well blended. Drop dough by rounded tablespoonfuls 2 inches apart onto prepared cookie sheets. Press remaining ⅓ cup toffee bits into dough mounds.

3. Bake 10 to 12 minutes or until set. Cool on cookie sheets 1 minute. Remove to wire racks; cool completely.

Makes about 24 cookies

Coconut Snowdrops

1 package (18 ounces)
   refrigerated chocolate
   chip cookie dough
¼ cup unsweetened cocoa
   powder
2 tablespoons brown sugar
2 cups toasted flaked
   coconut*
¾ cup marshmallow creme

*To toast, spread evenly on ungreased cookie sheet. Bake at 350°F 5 to 7 minutes, stirring often, until golden.

1. Preheat oven to 350°F. Grease cookie sheets. Let dough stand at room temperature 15 minutes. Beat cocoa and sugar with dough until blended.

2. Shape dough into 40 balls; place 1 inch apart on prepared cookie sheets. Bake 11 to 13 minutes or until puffed and slightly firm. Cool on cookie sheets 3 minutes. Remove to wire racks; cool completely.

3. Place toasted coconut on plate. Spread 1 rounded teaspoon marshmallow creme on each cookie; dip in coconut.

Makes 40 cookies

Toffee Chipsters

Fruity Oatmeal Jumbles

1 package (18 ounces) refrigerated oatmeal raisin cookie dough
¼ cup all-purpose flour
1 egg white
1 cup dried fruit bits (6-ounce package)
½ cup shelled pistachio nuts

1. Preheat oven to 350°F. Lightly grease cookie sheets. Let dough stand at room temperature about 15 minutes.

2. Combine dough, flour and egg white in large bowl; beat until well blended. Stir in fruit bits and pistachios. (Dough will be very sticky.) Drop dough by heaping tablespoonfuls 2 inches apart onto prepared cookie sheets.

3. Bake about 15 minutes or until edges are browned. Cool 2 minutes on cookie sheets. Remove to wire racks; cool completely.

Makes 18 cookies

Jammy Streusel Bars

1 package (18 ounces) refrigerated sugar cookie dough
½ cup jam (any flavor)
½ cup all-purpose flour
½ cup packed light brown sugar
¼ cup (½ stick) butter
1 cup sliced almonds or chopped walnuts

1. Preheat oven to 350°F. Grease 13×9-inch baking pan. Let dough stand at room temperature about 15 minutes.

2. Press dough evenly into prepared pan. Spread jam over dough; set aside.

3. Combine flour and brown sugar in medium bowl; cut in butter with pastry blender or two knives until mixture is crumbly. Sprinkle flour mixture over jam layer. Sprinkle evenly with almonds.

4. Bake 25 minutes or until lightly browned. Cool completely in pan on wire rack.

Makes 30 bars

Fruity Oatmeal Jumbles

Bodacious Bars

Tangy Lime Bars

  1 package (18 ounces) refrigerated sugar cookie dough
  ¾ cup all-purpose flour, divided
1¼ cups granulated sugar
  4 eggs
  ½ cup bottled key lime juice
  1 drop green food coloring
  1 teaspoon baking powder
    Powdered sugar

1. Preheat oven to 350°F. Lightly grease 13×9-inch baking pan. Let cookie dough stand at room temperature about 15 minutes.

2. Combine sugar cookie dough and ½ cup flour in large bowl; beat with electric mixer at medium speed until well blended. Press dough evenly onto bottom and ½ inch up sides of prepared pan. Bake 20 minutes.

continued on page 32

Tangy Lime Bars

Tangy Lime Bars, continued

3. Meanwhile, combine granulated sugar, eggs, lime juice and food coloring in large bowl; beat with electric mixer at high speed until well blended. Add remaining ¼ cup flour and baking powder; beat until well blended.

4. Pour over baked crust. Bake 18 to 21 minutes or until edges are browned and center is just set. Cool completely in pan on wire rack. Sprinkle with powdered sugar and cut into bars just before serving. Store leftovers covered in refrigerator.

Makes 24 bars

Jammy Wedges

1 package (18 ounces) refrigerated sugar cookie dough
¼ cup granulated sugar
1 egg
3 tablespoons blackberry jam
Powdered sugar
Additional blackberry jam (optional)

1. Preheat oven to 350°F. Lightly grease 9-inch glass pie plate; line bottom of plate with waxed paper. Let dough stand at room temperature about 15 minutes.

2. Combine cookie dough, granulated sugar and egg in large bowl; beat with electric mixer at medium speed until well blended. (Dough will be sticky.) Spread dough evenly in prepared pie plate; smooth top. Stir jam in small bowl until smooth. Dot top of dough with jam. Swirl jam into dough using tip of knife.

3. Bake 30 to 35 minutes or until edges are light brown and center is set. Cool at least 5 minutes in pie plate on wire rack.

4. Sprinkle with powdered sugar and cut into wedges just before serving. Serve with additional jam, if desired.

Makes 8 to 10 servings

Jammy Wedges

Banana Split Ice Cream Sandwiches

1 package (18 ounces) refrigerated chocolate chip cookie dough

2 ripe bananas, mashed

½ cup strawberry jam, divided

4 cups strawberry ice cream, softened

Hot fudge topping (optional)

Whipped cream (optional)

9 maraschino cherries (optional)

1. Preheat oven to 350°F. Lightly grease 13×9-inch baking pan. Let dough stand at room temperature about 15 minutes.

2. Combine dough and bananas in large bowl; beat with electric mixer at medium speed until well blended. Spread dough evenly into prepared pan; smooth top. Bake about 22 minutes or until edges are light brown. Cool completely in pan on wire rack.

3. Line 8×8-inch baking pan with aluminum foil or plastic wrap, allowing some to hang over edges of pan. Remove cooled cookie from pan; cut in half crosswise. Place 1 cookie half, top side down, in prepared pan, trimming edges to fit, if necessary. Spread ¼ cup jam evenly over cookie in pan. Spread ice cream evenly over jam. Spread remaining ¼ cup jam over bottom of remaining cookie half; place jam side down on ice cream. Cover tightly with foil or plastic wrap; freeze at least 2 hours or overnight.

4. Cut into bars and top with hot fudge sauce, whipped cream and cherries just before serving, if desired.

Makes 9 ice cream sandwiches

Banana Split Ice Cream Sandwiches

Peanut Butter Cookie Bars

1 package (18 ounces) refrigerated peanut butter cookie dough
1 can (14 ounces) sweetened condensed milk
¼ cup all-purpose flour
¼ cup peanut butter
1 cup peanut butter chips
1 cup chopped peanuts

1. Preheat oven to 350°F. Lightly grease 13×9-inch baking pan. Let cookie dough stand at room temperature about 15 minutes.

2. Press dough evenly onto bottom of prepared pan. Bake 10 minutes.

3. Meanwhile, combine sweetened condensed milk, flour and peanut butter in medium bowl; beat with electric mixer at medium speed until well blended. Spoon over partially baked crust. Sprinkle evenly with peanut butter chips and peanuts; press down lightly.

4. Bake 15 to 18 minutes or until center is set. Cool completely in pan on wire rack. Cut into bars to serve.

Makes about 24 bars

Unopened cans of sweetened condensed milk can be stored at room temperature for up to 6 months. Do not substitute evaporated milk, which is not sweet.

Peanut Butter Cookie Bars

Fruity Breakfast Bars

1 package (18 ounces) refrigerated oatmeal raisin cookie dough
1/3 cup uncooked old-fashioned oats
1 egg
2 tablespoons honey
1/3 cup chopped dried apricots or chopped dried mango
1/3 cup dried cranberries
1/3 cup dried cherries
1/4 cup sunflower kernels

1. Preheat oven to 350°F. Lightly grease 11×7-inch baking pan. Let cookie dough stand at room temperature about 15 minutes.

2. Combine oatmeal raisin cookie dough, uncooked old-fashioned oats, egg and honey in large bowl; beat with electric mixer at medium speed until well blended.

3. Combine chopped dried apricots, dried cranberries, dried cherries and sunflower kernels in medium bowl. Add dried fruit mixture to cookie dough mixture; stir until well blended. Press dough evenly into prepared baking pan.

4. Bake 25 to 30 minutes or until edges are brown and toothpick inserted into center comes out clean. Cool completely in pan on wire rack. Cut into bars to serve.

Makes 16 bars

Fruity Breakfast Bars

Cheesecake Cookie Bars

2 packages (18 ounces each) refrigerated chocolate chip cookie dough

2 packages (8 ounces each) cream cheese, softened

½ cup sugar

2 eggs

1. Preheat oven to 350°F. Lightly grease 13×9-inch baking pan. Let both packages of cookie dough stand at room temperature about 15 minutes.

2. Reserve three fourths of one package of dough. Press remaining one and one-fourth packages of dough evenly onto bottom of prepared pan.

3. Combine softened cream cheese, sugar and eggs in large bowl; beat with electric mixer at high speed until well blended and smooth. Spread cream cheese mixture evenly over cookie dough in pan.

Break reserved three fourths package of cookie dough into small pieces; sprinkle evenly over cream cheese mixture.

4. Bake 35 minutes or until center is almost set. Cool completely in pan on wire rack. Cut into bars to serve. Store leftovers covered in refrigerator.

Makes about 24 bars

To soften cream cheese quickly, unwrap it and place it on a microwavable plate. Microwave on MEDIUM (50%) 15 to 20 seconds or until slightly softened.

Cheesecake Cookie Bars

Banana Oatmeal Snack Bars

2 packages (18 ounces each) refrigerated oatmeal raisin cookie dough
2 bananas, mashed
3 eggs
½ teaspoon ground cinnamon
1 cup uncooked old-fashioned oats
1 cup dried cranberries
½ cup chopped dried apricots
½ cup chopped pecans
   Powdered sugar

1. Preheat oven to 350°F. Lightly grease 13×9-inch baking pan. Let both packages of cookie dough stand at room temperature about 15 minutes.

2. Combine cookie dough, mashed bananas, eggs and ground cinnamon in large bowl; beat with electric mixer at high speed until well blended.

3. Combine uncooked old-fashioned oats, dried cranberries, chopped dried apricots and chopped pecans in medium bowl; stir until blended. Stir fruit and oat mixture into cookie dough until well blended. Spread dough evenly in prepared pan; smooth top.

4. Bake 40 to 45 minutes or until top is browned and toothpick inserted into center comes out clean. Cool completely in pan on wire rack.

5. Sprinkle with powdered sugar and cut into bars just before serving.

Makes about 24 bars

Banana Oatmeal Snack Bars

Taffy Apple Bars

1 package (18 ounces)
   refrigerated sugar
   cookie dough
1 package (18 ounces)
   refrigerated peanut
   butter cookie dough
½ cup all-purpose flour
2 large apples, cored,
   peeled and chopped
   (3½ to 4 cups)
1 cup chopped peanuts
½ cup caramel ice cream
   topping

1. Preheat oven to 350°F. Lightly grease 13×9-inch baking pan. Let both packages of cookie dough stand at room temperature about 15 minutes.

2. Combine sugar cookie dough, peanut butter cookie dough and flour in large bowl; beat with electric mixer at medium speed until well blended. Press dough evenly onto bottom of prepared pan. Spoon apples evenly over dough; press down lightly. Sprinkle with peanuts.

3. Bake about 35 minutes or until edges are browned and center is set. Cool completely in pan on wire rack. Drizzle with caramel topping. Cut into bars to serve.

Makes about 24 bars

Crisp, tart, juicy Granny Smith apples are not only delicious eaten raw, but are also excellent for baking because they keep their texture.

Taffy Apple Bars

Pecan Pie Bars

1 package (18 ounces) refrigerated sugar cookie dough
½ cup all-purpose flour
3 eggs
¾ cup dark corn syrup
¾ cup sugar
1 teaspoon vanilla
¼ teaspoon salt
3 cups chopped pecans

1. Preheat oven to 350°F. Lightly grease 13×9-inch baking pan. Let cookie dough stand at room temperature about 15 minutes.

2. Combine cookie dough and flour in large bowl; beat with electric mixer at medium speed until well blended. Press dough evenly onto bottom and ½ inch up sides of prepared pan. Bake 20 minutes.

3. Meanwhile, beat eggs in large bowl with electric mixer at high speed until fluffy and light in color. Add dark corn syrup, sugar, vanilla and salt; beat until well blended. Pour egg mixture over partially baked crust; sprinkle evenly with chopped pecans.

4. Bake 25 to 30 minutes or until center is just set. Cool completely in pan on wire rack. Cut into bars to serve.

Makes about 24 bars

Pecans can be stored in an airtight container up to 3 months in the refrigerator and up to 6 months in the freezer.

Pecan Pie Bars

Oatmeal Date Bars

2 packages (18 ounces each) refrigerated oatmeal raisin cookie dough
2½ cups uncooked old-fashioned oats, divided
2 packages (8 ounces each) chopped dates
1 cup water
½ cup sugar
1 teaspoon vanilla

1. Preheat oven to 350°F. Lightly grease 13×9-inch baking pan. Let both packages of cookie dough stand at room temperature about 15 minutes.

2. For topping, combine three fourths of one package of cookie dough and 1 cup uncooked oats in medium bowl; beat with electric mixer at medium speed until well blended. Set aside.

3. For crust, combine remaining one and one fourth packages of dough and remaining 1½ cups uncooked oats in large bowl; beat with electric mixer at medium speed until well blended. Press dough evenly onto bottom of prepared pan. Bake 10 minutes.

4. Meanwhile for filling, combine chopped dates, water and sugar in medium saucepan; bring to a boil over high heat. Boil 3 minutes; remove from heat and stir in vanilla. Spread date mixture evenly over partially baked crust; sprinkle evenly with topping mixture.

5. Bake 25 to 28 minutes or until bubbly. Cool completely in pan on wire rack. Cut into bars to serve.

Makes about 24 bars

Oatmeal Date Bars

Chocolate Temptations

Spicy Oatmeal Combos

1 package (18 ounces) refrigerated sugar cookie dough
1 package (18 ounces) refrigerated oatmeal raisin cookie dough
¼ cup unsweetened cocoa powder
1¼ teaspoons ground ginger

1. Preheat oven to 350°F. Lightly grease cookie sheets. Let both packages of dough stand at room temperature about 15 minutes.

2. Combine sugar dough, cocoa and ginger in large bowl; beat until well blended. Gently stir in oatmeal dough just until marbled. (Do not mix doughs thoroughly.) Shape dough into ¾-inch balls; place 2 inches apart on prepared cookie sheets.

3. Bake 8 to 10 minutes or until edges are lightly browned. Cool 2 minutes on cookie sheets. Remove to wire racks; cool completely.

Makes 48 cookies

Spicy Oatmeal Combos

Black Forest Tarts

- **1 package (18 ounces) refrigerated triple chocolate cookie dough**
- **¹⁄₃ cup unsweetened cocoa powder**
- **1 can (21 ounces) cherry pie filling**
- **3 squares (1 ounce each) white chocolate, finely chopped**

1. Preheat oven to 350°F. Lightly grease 18 standard (2¹⁄₂-inch) muffin pan cups or line with paper or foil baking cups. Let cookie dough stand at room temperature about 15 minutes.

2. Combine cookie dough and cocoa in large bowl; beat until well blended. Shape dough into 18 balls; press onto bottoms and up sides of prepared muffin cups.

3. Bake about 15 minutes or until set. Remove from oven; gently press down center of each cookie cup with back of teaspoon. Cool in pan 10 minutes. Remove cookie cups from pans; cool completely on wire rack.

4. Place 1 tablespoon cherry pie filling in each cookie cup.

5. Place white chocolate in small resealable food storage bag. Microwave on MEDIUM (50%) 1 minute; knead bag lightly. Microwave and knead at additional 30-second intervals until white chocolate is completely melted. Cut off tiny corner of bag. Drizzle white chocolate over tarts. Let stand until set.

Makes 18 tarts

Black Forest Tarts

Turtle Brownies

- **1 package (18 ounces) refrigerated sugar cookie dough**
- **⅓ cup unsweetened cocoa powder**
- **1 egg, lightly beaten**
- **10 caramels**
- **2 tablespoons whipping cream**
- **1 cup coarsely chopped pecans**

1. Preheat oven to 350°F. Lightly grease 11×7-inch baking pan. Let cookie dough stand at room temperature about 15 minutes.

2. Combine cookie dough, cocoa and egg in large bowl; beat at medium speed of electric mixer until well blended. (Dough will be sticky.) Press dough evenly onto bottom of prepared pan. Bake 12 minutes.

3. Meanwhile, place caramels and cream in small microwavable bowl.

Microwave on HIGH 3 minutes or until caramels are soft; stir until mixture is smooth.

4. Remove brownies from oven. Drop spoonfuls of caramel mixture over top; sprinkle with pecans. Bake additional 8 to 9 minutes or until center is set. Cool completely in pan on wire rack.   *Makes 15 brownies*

Warm nuts are easier to chop than cold nuts. Place 1 cup of shelled nuts in a microwavable dish; heat on HIGH about 30 seconds or just until warm; chop as desired.

Turtle Brownies

Mint Chip Thumbprints

2 packages (18 ounces each) refrigerated miniature chocolate chip cookie dough

⅓ cup all-purpose flour

½ teaspoon peppermint extract

1 box (5 ounces) miniature (¾-inch) chocolate-covered mint candies

1. Preheat oven to 350°F. Lightly grease cookie sheets. Let both packages of dough stand at room temperature about 15 minutes.

2. Combine both doughs, flour and peppermint extract in large bowl; beat until blended. Shape dough into 1-inch balls; place 2 inches apart on prepared cookie sheets.

3. Bake 5 minutes. Press one candy into each dough ball. Bake additional 4 to 6 minutes or until edges are lightly browned. Cool 2 minutes on cookie sheets. Remove to wire racks; cool completely.

Makes about 42 cookies

Chocolate Crunchies

1 package (18 ounces) refrigerated sugar cookie dough

½ cup unsweetened cocoa powder

1 egg

3 bars (1.55 ounces each) milk chocolate with crisp rice candy, chopped

1. Preheat oven to 350°F. Lightly grease cookie sheets. Let dough stand at room temperature about 15 minutes.

2. Combine dough, cocoa and egg in large bowl; beat until well blended. Stir in candy. Shape dough into ¾-inch balls; place 2 inches apart on prepared cookie sheets.

3. Bake 7 to 9 minutes or until set. Cool on cookie sheets 1 minute. Remove to wire racks; cool completely.

Makes about 36 cookies

Mint Chip Thumbprints

Black & White Bars

- **1 package (18 ounces) refrigerated sugar cookie dough**
- **1 package (18 ounces) refrigerated triple chocolate cookie dough**
- **2 squares (1 ounce each) white chocolate, finely chopped**

1. Lightly grease 11×7-inch baking pan. Let both packages of cookie dough stand at room temperature about 15 minutes.

2. Preheat oven to 350°F. Press sugar cookie dough evenly onto bottom of prepared pan. Freeze 15 minutes.

3. Press triple chocolate cookie dough evenly over sugar dough in pan. Bake 37 to 40 minutes or until edges are browned and center is set. Cool completely in pan on wire rack.

4. Place white chocolate in small resealable food storage bag. Microwave on MEDIUM (50%) 1 minute; knead bag lightly. Microwave and knead at additional 30-second intervals until white chocolate is completely melted. Cut off tiny corner of bag. Drizzle white chocolate over bars. Let stand until set.

Makes 12 bars

White chocolate is not real chocolate because it lacks chocolate liquor. It is more delicate than other chocolates and burns easily, so be very careful when melting it.

Black & White Bars

S'More Cups

- **1 package (18 ounces) refrigerated miniature chocolate chip cookie dough**
- **1 cup graham cracker crumbs**
- **1²/₃ cups semisweet chocolate chips**
- **1 cup whipping cream**
- **1 package (10 ounces) miniature marshmallows**
- **Bear-shaped graham crackers**

1. Preheat oven to 350°F. Lightly grease 18 standard (2½-inch) muffin pan cups or line with paper or foil baking cups. Let cookie dough stand at room temperature about 15 minutes.

2. Combine dough and cracker crumbs in large bowl; beat until well blended. Shape dough into 18 balls; press onto bottoms and up sides of prepared muffin cups.

3. Bake 12 to 15 minutes or until set. Remove from oven; gently press down center of each cookie cup with back of teaspoon. Cool in pans 10 minutes. Remove cups from pans; cool completely on wire rack.

4. Place chocolate chips in large bowl. Place cream in small saucepan; bring to a boil over medium heat. Pour hot cream over chocolate chips; stir until chocolate is melted and mixture is smooth. Cool 5 minutes. Meanwhile, preheat broiler.

5. Place cookie cups on ungreased cookie sheet. Divide cooled chocolate mixture evenly among cookie cups. Place 7 marshmallows on top of each cup. Broil cookie cups 20 to 30 seconds or until marshmallows are golden brown. Garnish with bear-shaped graham crackers.

Makes 18 cups

S'More Cups

Chocolate Cherry Gems

- **1 package (18 ounces) refrigerated sugar cookie dough**
- **⅓ cup unsweetened Dutch process cocoa powder***
- **3 tablespoons maraschino cherry juice, divided**
- **18 maraschino cherries, cut into halves**
- **¾ cup powdered sugar**

The Dutch process, or European-style, cocoa gives these cookies an intense chocolate flavor and a dark, rich color. Other unsweetened cocoas can be substituted, but the flavor may be milder and the color may be lighter.

1. Preheat oven to 350°F. Lightly grease cookie sheets. Let dough stand at room temperature about 15 minutes.

2. Combine cookie dough, cocoa and 1 tablespoon cherry juice in large bowl; beat at medium speed of electric mixer until well blended. Shape dough into ¾-inch balls; place 2 inches apart on prepared cookie sheets.

3. Flatten balls slightly; press cherry half into center of each ball.

4. Bake 9 to 11 minutes or until set. Cool 2 minutes on cookie sheets. Remove to wire racks; cool completely.

5. Combine powdered sugar and remaining 2 tablespoons cherry juice in small bowl; whisk until smooth and well blended. Add additional cherry juice, 1 teaspoon at a time, if necessary, to make medium-thick pourable glaze. Drizzle glaze over cooled cookies. Let stand until set.

Makes 36 cookies

Chocolate Cherry Gems

Chocolate Almond Sandwiches

**1 package (18 ounces)
refrigerated sugar
cookie dough**
4 ounces almond paste
¼ cup all-purpose flour
**1 container (16 ounces)
dark chocolate
frosting**
Sliced almonds

1. Let cookie dough stand at room temperature about 15 minutes.

2. Combine cookie dough, almond paste and flour in large bowl; beat until well blended. Divide dough into 3 pieces; freeze 20 minutes. On waxed paper or plastic wrap, shape each piece into 10×1-inch log. Wrap tightly in plastic wrap; refrigerate at least 2 hours or overnight. (Or freeze about 1 hour or until firm.)

3. Preheat oven to 350°F. Lightly grease cookie sheets. Cut dough into ³⁄₈-inch slices; place 2 inches apart on prepared cookie sheets.

4. Bake 10 to 12 minutes or until edges are lightly browned. Cool 2 minutes on cookie sheets. Remove to wire racks; cool completely.

5. Spread scant 2 teaspoons frosting each on bottoms of half the cookies; top with remaining cookies. Place dab of frosting and sliced almond on top of each sandwich cookie.

Makes 30 sandwich cookies

Note: Almond paste is a prepared product made of ground blanched almonds, sugar and an ingredient, such as glucose, glycerin or corn syrup, to keep it pliable. It is often used to as an ingredient in confections and baked goods. Almond paste is available in cans and plastic tubes in most supermarkets or gourmet food markets. After opening, wrap the container tightly and store it in the refrigerator.

*Chocolate Almond
Sandwiches*

Tiny Hot Fudge Sundae Cups

1 package (18 ounces) refrigerated sugar cookie dough

⅓ cup unsweetened cocoa powder

5 to 7 cups vanilla ice cream

Hot fudge ice cream topping, colored sprinkles and aerosol whipped topping

9 maraschino cherries, cut into quarters

1. Preheat oven to 350°F. Spray outsides of 36 mini (1¾-inch) muffin pan cups with nonstick cooking spray. Let cookie dough stand at room temperature about 15 minutes.

2. Combine cookie dough and cocoa in large bowl; beat until well blended. Divide dough into 36 equal pieces; shape each piece over outside of prepared muffin pan cup. Bake 10 to 12 minutes or until set. Cool on pans 10 minutes. Remove cups from pans; cool completely on wire racks.

3. Fill each cooled cookie cup with 2 to 3 tablespoons ice cream. Drizzle with hot fudge sauce; top with sprinkles. Garnish each sundae cup with whipped topping and cherry quarter.

Makes 36 sundae cups

Unsweetened cocoa powder can be stored in a tightly closed container in a cool, dark place for up to two years.

Tiny Hot Fudge Sundae Cups

Buckeye Buttons

2 packages (18 ounces each) refrigerated triple chocolate cookie dough

½ (18-ounce) package refrigerated peanut butter cookie dough*

1 cup chopped peanuts

½ cup chocolate chips

36 peanut halves and additional chopped peanuts (optional)

Save remaining ½ package of dough for another use.

1. Preheat oven to 350°F. Lightly grease 13×9-inch baking pan. Let both packages of chocolate dough stand at room temperature about 15 minutes.

2. Press both packages of chocolate dough evenly onto bottom of prepared pan. Cut half package of peanut butter dough into ¼-inch slices. Place slices on top of chocolate dough in pan, spacing evenly. Sprinkle with chopped peanuts; press down lightly.

3. Bake 25 to 30 minutes or until toothpick inserted into center comes out clean. Cool completely in pan on wire rack.

4. Cut bars into "buttons" using 1½-inch round cookie cutter. Place buttons on wire rack set over waxed paper.

5. Place chocolate chips in small microwavable bowl. Microwave on HIGH 30 seconds; stir. Repeat as necessary until chips are melted. Drizzle melted chocolate over rounds; top each round with peanut half and chopped peanuts, if desired. Let stand until set.

Makes about 36 cookies

Buckeye Buttons

Fudgy Chocolate Padgies

2 packages (18 ounces each) refrigerated triple chocolate cookie dough
½ cup all-purpose flour
½ cup unsweetened Dutch process cocoa powder*
2 egg whites
1 cup chopped cashews

*The Dutch process, or European-style, cocoa gives these cookies an intense chocolate flavor and a dark, rich color. Other unsweetened cocoas can be substituted, but the flavor may be milder and the color may be lighter.

1. Preheat oven to 350°F. Lightly grease cookie sheets. Let both packages of dough stand at room temperature about 15 minutes.

2. Combine both doughs, flour, cocoa and egg whites in large bowl; beat with electric mixer at medium speed until well blended. Stir in cashews.

3. Drop dough by heaping tablespoonfuls 2 inches apart onto prepared cookie sheets. Bake 10 to 12 minutes or until centers are set. Cool 2 minutes on cookie sheets. Remove to wire racks; cool completely.

Makes about 36 cookies

To separate an egg, break it in half over a bowl. Holding a shell half in each hand, transfer the yolk back and forth between the shell halves, allowing the white to drip into the bowl.

Fudgy Chocolate Padgies

Just For Fun

Sparkling Magic Wands

1 package (18 ounces) refrigerated sugar cookie dough
48 pretzel sticks (2½ inches long)
    Prepared colored decorating icings
    Colored sugar or edible glitter and gold dragées

1. Preheat oven to 350°F.

2. Roll dough to ⅛-inch thickness on well-floured surface. Cut dough with 2-inch star-shaped cookie cutter. Place each star on top of 1 pretzel stick; press lightly to attach. Place on ungreased cookie sheet.

3. Bake 4 to 6 minutes or until edges are lightly browned. Carefully remove to wire racks; cool completely.

4. Spread icing on stars; sprinkle with colored sugar. Press dragées into points of stars. Let stand until set.

Makes 48 cookies

Pretty Posies

1 package (18 ounces) refrigerated sugar cookie dough

Orange and blue or purple food colorings

1 tablespoon colored sprinkles

1. Let dough stand at room temperature about 15 minutes.

2. Combine one sixth of dough, orange food coloring and sprinkles in small bowl; beat until well blended. Shape into 7½-inch-long log. Wrap in plastic wrap; refrigerate 30 minutes or until firm.

3. Combine remaining dough and blue food coloring in large bowl; beat until well blended. Shape dough into disc. Wrap in plastic wrap; refrigerate 30 minutes or until firm.

4. Roll out blue dough between sheets of waxed paper into 7½×6-inch rectangle. Remove top sheet of waxed paper. Place orange log in center of blue rectangle. Fold blue edges up and around orange log; press seam together. Roll gently to form smooth log. Wrap waxed paper around dough; twist ends to secure. Freeze log 20 minutes.

5. Preheat oven to 350°F. Lightly grease cookie sheets. Cut log into ¼-inch slices. Place 2 inches apart on prepared cookie sheets. Using 2½-inch flower-shaped cookie cutter, cut slices into flowers; remove and discard dough scraps.

6. Bake 15 to 17 minutes or until edges are lightly browned. Remove to wire racks; cool completely.

Makes about 18 cookies

Pretty Posies

Citrus Slices

1 package (18 ounces) refrigerated sugar cookie dough

3 tablespoons all-purpose flour

½ teaspoon lemon extract

½ teaspoon lime extract

½ teaspoon orange extract

Yellow, green and orange food coloring

Yellow, green and orange decorating sugars

1 egg white, lightly beaten

Coarse white decorating sugar

1. Let dough stand at room temperature about 15 minutes.

2. Combine dough and flour in large bowl; beat until well blended. Divide dough into 3 equal pieces. Add lemon extract and yellow food coloring to one dough piece in medium bowl; beat until well blended. Shape lemon dough into 6×1½-inch log; flatten one side of log so that log has half-moon shape. Brush rounded side of log with egg white; sprinkle with yellow sugar until evenly coated. Wrap tightly in plastic wrap; freeze 1 hour. Repeat with second piece of dough, lime extract, green food coloring and green sugar. Repeat with remaining piece of dough, orange extract, orange food coloring and orange sugar.

3. Preheat oven to 350°F. Lightly grease cookie sheets. Cut logs into ¼-inch slices; place 2 inches apart on prepared cookie sheets. Sprinkle with coarse white sugar.

4. Bake 9 to 11 minutes or until set. Working quickly, score segment lines on hot cookies. Cool on cookie sheets 2 minutes. Remove to wire racks; cool completely.

Makes about 60 cookies

Citrus Slices

Birthday Cake Cookies

1 package (18 ounces) refrigerated sugar cookie dough
1 container (16 ounces) prepared white frosting
Food coloring (optional)
Colored sprinkles or decors
10 small birthday candles

1. Preheat oven to 350°F. Lightly grease 10 mini (1¾-inch) muffin pan cups and 10 standard (2½-inch) muffin pan cups. Shape one third of dough into 10 (1-inch) balls; press onto bottoms and up sides of prepared mini muffin cups. Shape remaining two thirds of dough into 10 equal balls; press onto bottoms and up sides of prepared standard muffin cups.

2. Bake mini cookies 8 to 9 minutes or until edges are lightly browned. Bake regular cookies 10 to 11 minutes or until edges are lightly browned. Cool 5 minutes in pans on wire racks. Remove cookies to wire racks; cool completely.

3. Add food coloring, if desired, to frosting; mix well. Spread frosting over top and side of each cookie. Place 1 mini cookie on top of 1 regular cookie. Decorate with sprinkles. Press 1 candle into center of each cookie.

Makes 10 cookie cakes

Food colorings are edible dyes used to tint frostings and candies. They impart intense color and should initially be used sparingly, a drop or two at a time.

Birthday Cake Cookies

Zebras

2 packages (18 ounces each) refrigerated sugar cookie dough
½ cup all-purpose flour
½ cup unsweetened Dutch process cocoa powder
Prepared dark chocolate frosting
Sprinkles
Mini chocolate chips and regular chocolate chips

1. Let dough stand at room temperature about 15 minutes.

2. Mix 1 dough package and flour in large bowl; beat until blended. Mix remaining dough and cocoa in another large bowl; beat until blended. Wrap doughs separately in plastic wrap; freeze 15 minutes.

3. Roll each flavor of dough separately into 9-inch square between lightly floured pieces of waxed paper. Remove waxed paper. Place cocoa dough on top of plain dough. Cut into four 4½-inch squares. Layer squares on top of each other, alternating cocoa and plain doughs, to make one stack. Wrap in plastic wrap; refrigerate at least 4 hours or up to 2 days.

4. Preheat oven to 350°F. Grease cookie sheets. Cut dough into ¼-inch slices (wipe off knife after each cut). Cut slices in half into 2¼×2-inch rectangles; place 2 inches apart on prepared cookie sheets.

5. With stripes vertical, for each zebra, cut small triangle from top left corner and narrow triangle from top right edge (diagram 1 on page 82); discard. Cut small triangle from center of bottom; place at top of cookie for ear (diagram 2 on page 82).

6. Bake 10 minutes or until edges are lightly browned. Cool on cookie sheets 5 minutes. Remove to wire racks; cool completely.

7. Spread frosting on edges at sides of ears; top with sprinkles. With frosting, attach 1 mini chocolate chip for eye and 1 regular chocolate chip for nostril.

Makes 36 cookies

continued on page 82

Zebras

Zebras, continued

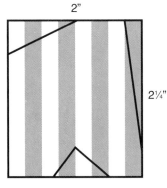

2"

2¼"

Diagram 1

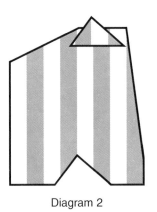

Diagram 2

Tie-Dyed T-Shirts

**1 package (18 ounces)
refrigerated sugar
cookie dough**
**6 tablespoons all-purpose
flour, divided**
**Red, yellow and blue food
colorings**

1. Let dough stand at room
temperature about 15 minutes.

2. Divide dough into
3 pieces; place in separate
medium bowls. Add
2 tablespoons flour and red
food coloring to dough in
one bowl; beat until well
blended and evenly colored.
Wrap in plastic wrap;
refrigerate 20 minutes. Repeat
with second dough piece,
2 tablespoons flour and
yellow food coloring. Repeat
with remaining dough piece,
remaining 2 tablespoons flour
and blue food coloring.

3. Preheat oven to 350°F.
Lightly grease cookie sheets.
Divide each color dough in
half. Press together half of
yellow dough with half of red
dough. Roll dough on lightly

floured surface to ¼-inch thickness. Cut dough with 3-inch t-shirt-shaped cookie cutter or use pattern (see page 6). Place cutouts 2 inches apart on prepared cookie sheets. Repeat with remaining dough, pairing remaining yellow dough with half of blue dough and remaining red dough with remaining blue dough.

4. Bake 7 to 9 minutes or until firm but not browned. Cool completely on cookie sheets.

Makes about 18 cookies

Nothin' But Net

- **1 package (18 ounces) refrigerated sugar cookie dough**
- **1¼ cups all-purpose flour**
- **2 tablespoons powdered sugar**
- **2 tablespoons fresh lemon juice**
- **Orange, white and black decorating icing**

1. Let dough stand at room temperature about 15 minutes.

2. Combine dough, flour, powdered sugar and lemon juice in large bowl; beat until well blended. Divide dough in half. Wrap each half in plastic wrap; refrigerate at least 2 hours.

3. Meanwhile, draw pattern for cookies on cardboard, using back cover photo; cut out pattern (see page 6).

4. Preheat oven to 350°F. Lightly grease cookie sheets. Roll one dough half to ¼-inch thickness on lightly floured surface. Place pattern on dough. Cut dough around pattern with sharp knife. Place cutouts 2 inches apart on prepared cookie sheets. Repeat with remaining dough half.

5. Bake 13 to 15 minutes or until edges are lightly browned. Remove to wire racks; cool completely.

6. Decorate with icings like a basket ball net as shown on back cover photo.

Makes 18 cookies

Roaring Campfires

1 package (18 ounces) refrigerated peanut butter cookie dough
¾ cup all-purpose flour
2 tablespoons unsweetened cocoa powder
2 cups broken thin pretzel sticks
1 tube (4.25 ounces) yellow decorator icing with decorating tip
1 tube (4.25 ounces) orange decorator icing with decorating tip

1. Preheat oven to 350°F. Lightly grease cookie sheets. Let cookie dough stand at room temperature about 15 minutes.

2. Combine cookie dough, flour and cocoa powder in large bowl; beat with electric mixer at medium speed until well blended. Shape dough into 1-inch balls; place 2 inches apart on prepared cookie sheets.

3. Bake about 7 minutes or until set. Immediately press pretzel pieces into sides of cookies to resemble campfire logs. Carefully remove to wire racks; cool completely.

4. Using decorating tips, pipe yellow and orange icing onto cooled cookies to resemble flames.

Makes about 36 cookies

To accurately measure dry ingredients, always use standardized measuring spoons and cups. Fill the measuring spoon or cup to overflowing and level it off with a knife.

Snickerpoodles

- **1 package (18 ounces) refrigerated sugar cookie dough**
- **1 teaspoon ground cinnamon, divided**
- **1 teaspoon vanilla**
- **¼ cup sugar**
- **Chocolate chips**
- **Prepared white icing**
- **Miniature chocolate chips**
- **Prepared colored icing (optional)**

1. Preheat oven to 350°F. Lightly grease cookie sheets. Let dough stand at room temperature about 15 minutes.

2. Combine dough, ½ teaspoon cinnamon and vanilla in large bowl; beat until well blended. Combine sugar and remaining ½ teaspoon cinnamon in small bowl. For each poodle face, shape ½ tablespoon dough into oval. Roll in cinnamon-sugar; place on prepared cookie sheet. For poodle ears, divide ½ tablespoon dough in half; shape each half into teardrop shape. Roll in cinnamon-sugar; place on cookie sheet at either side of face. For top of poodle head, shape scant teaspoon dough into oval. Roll in cinnamon-sugar; place on cookie sheet at top of face.

3. Bake 10 to 12 minutes or until edges are lightly browned. Immediately press 1 chocolate chip upside down in face for nose. Cool 2 minutes on cookie sheets. Remove to wire racks; cool completely.

4. Pipe small dots of white icing on cookies and place mini chocolate chips upside down in icing for eyes. Decorate with white and colored icings, if desired. Let stand until set.

Makes about 24 cookies

Snickerpoodles

Lollipop Flower Pots

1 package (18 ounces) refrigerated sugar cookie dough

36 caramels

1 cup chocolate cookie crumbs

36 small lollipops

Green gummy candy spearmint leaves

Prepared green icing (optional)

1. Preheat oven to 350°F. Lightly grease 36 mini (1¾-inch) muffin pan cups or line with paper baking cups. Shape sugar cookie dough into 36 balls; press onto bottoms and up sides of prepared muffin cups. Place 1 caramel in center of each muffin cup.

2. Bake 10 to 11 minutes or until edges are lightly browned. Cool cookies in pans on wire racks. Remove to wire racks; cool completely.

3. Sprinkle heaping 1 teaspoon cookie crumbs into center of each cookie. Carefully push 1 lollipop into each cookie cup. Press candy spearmint leaves into cookies. Use dab of icing to help make spearmint candies stand up, if necessary.

Makes 36 cookies

These colorful cookies make great place cards for parties. Simply write each guest's name in white icing on a lollipop before inserting it into the cookie.

Lollipop Flower Pots

Marshmallow Ice Cream Cone Cookies

1 package (18 ounces) refrigerated sugar cookie dough

6 ice cream sugar cones, broken into pieces

1 container (16 ounces) prepared white frosting

1 package (10.5 ounces) colored miniature marshmallows

Colored sprinkles

1. Preheat oven to 350°F. Let cookie dough stand at room temperature about 15 minutes.

2. Meanwhile, place sugar cones in bowl of food processor. Process using on/off pulses until finely ground. Combine cookie dough and ground sugar cones in large bowl; beat until well blended.

3. Shape dough into 3 equal balls. Pat each ball into 9-inch circle on lightly floured surface. Cut each circle into 6 wedges; place wedges 2 inches apart on ungreased cookie sheets.

4. Bake 10 to 11 minutes or until edges are lightly browned. While cookies are still warm, score criss-cross pattern into cookies with dull side of knife. Cool on cookie sheets 5 minutes. Remove cookies to wire racks; cool completely.

5. For each cookie, spread 2-inch strip of frosting at wide end. Press about $\frac{1}{3}$ cup marshmallows onto frosting and decorate with sprinkles.

Makes 18 cookies

Marshmallow Ice Cream
Cone Cookies

Peppermint Pigs

1 package (18 ounces) refrigerated sugar cookie dough

½ cup all-purpose flour

¾ teaspoon peppermint extract

Red food coloring

Prepared white icing and mini candy-coated chocolate pieces

1. Preheat oven to 350°F. Lightly grease cookie sheets. Let cookie dough stand at room temperature about 15 minutes.

2. Combine dough, flour, peppermint extract and food coloring in large bowl; beat until well blended and evenly colored. Divide dough into 20 equal pieces. For each pig, shape 1 dough piece into one 1-inch ball, one ½-inch ball and two ¼-inch balls. Flatten 1-inch ball to ¼-inch-thick round; place on prepared cookie sheet. Flatten ½-inch ball to ¼-inch-thick oval; place on top of dough round for snout. Shape two ¼-inch balls into triangles; fold point over and place at top of round for ears. Make indentations in snout for nostrils with toothpick.

3. Bake 9 to 11 minutes or until set. Remove to wire racks; cool completely. Pipe small dots of white icing on cookies and place candy-coated chocolate pieces in icing for eyes.

Makes 20 cookies

Small amounts of extracts, usually 1 teaspoon or less, provide lots of flavor without adding moisture.

Index

Index

Metric Conversion Chart

VOLUME MEASUREMENTS (dry)

1/8 teaspoon = 0.5 mL
1/4 teaspoon = 1 mL
1/2 teaspoon = 2 mL
3/4 teaspoon = 4 mL
1 teaspoon = 5 mL
1 tablespoon = 15 mL
2 tablespoons = 30 mL
1/4 cup = 60 mL
1/3 cup = 75 mL
1/2 cup = 125 mL
2/3 cup = 150 mL
3/4 cup = 175 mL
1 cup = 250 mL
2 cups = 1 pint = 500 mL
3 cups = 750 mL
4 cups = 1 quart = 1 L

VOLUME MEASUREMENTS (fluid)

1 fluid ounce (2 tablespoons) = 30 mL
4 fluid ounces (1/2 cup) = 125 mL
8 fluid ounces (1 cup) = 250 mL
12 fluid ounces (1 1/2 cups) = 375 mL
16 fluid ounces (2 cups) = 500 mL

WEIGHTS (mass)

1/2 ounce = 15 g
1 ounce = 30 g
3 ounces = 90 g
4 ounces = 120 g
8 ounces = 225 g
10 ounces = 285 g
12 ounces = 360 g
16 ounces = 1 pound = 450 g

DIMENSIONS

1/16 inch = 2 mm
1/8 inch = 3 mm
1/4 inch = 6 mm
1/2 inch = 1.5 cm
3/4 inch = 2 cm
1 inch = 2.5 cm

OVEN TEMPERATURES

250°F = 120°C
275°F = 140°C
300°F = 150°C
325°F = 160°C
350°F = 180°C
375°F = 190°C
400°F = 200°C
425°F = 220°C
450°F = 230°C

BAKING PAN SIZES

Utensil	Size in Inches/Quarts	Metric Volume	Size in Centimeters
Baking or Cake Pan (square or rectangular)	8×8×2	2 L	20×20×5
	9×9×2	2.5 L	23×23×5
	12×8×2	3 L	30×20×5
	13×9×2	3.5 L	33×23×5
Loaf Pan	8×4×3	1.5 L	20×10×7
	9×5×3	2 L	23×13×7
Round Layer Cake Pan	8×1½	1.2 L	20×4
	9×1½	1.5 L	23×4
Pie Plate	8×1¼	750 mL	20×3
	9×1¼	1 L	23×3
Baking Dish or Casserole	1 quart	1 L	—
	1½ quart	1.5 L	—
	2 quart	2 L	—